Three Crises in American Foreign Affairs and a Continuing Revolution

HOWARD TRIVERS

Southern Illinois University Press

CARBONDALE AND EDWARDSVILLE

Feffer & Simons, Inc., London & Amsterdam

To
M. R. T.
and
The Seven – A Happy Number

CONTENTS

ACKNOWLEDGMENTS

This book is a collection of four essays based on public lectures given at Southern Illinois University during the period November 1969 to January 1971. The lectures on the Berlin Wall, the Cuba missile crisis, and Vietnam were given under the auspices of the Government Department or the International Relations Club of the University, to whom I am indebted for their sponsorship. These three essays are based considerably on the direct personal experience and involvement of the author, particularly in the cases of the Berlin Wall and the Cuba missile crisis, and represent the effort of a retired Foreign Service officer to reflect on the foreign policy implications in each case. The essay "The Continuing Revolution: Science, Technology, and Foreign Affairs" was first presented as a double-length public lecture at Southern Illinois University in a multidisciplinary General Studies course entitled "War and Peace Studies." The length of the present essay reflects in part the original double length of the lecture; however, it also reflects the fact that the subject is inexhaustible; indeed, many pertinent topics were eliminated in order to hold this essay to its present dimension.

The first three essays deal primarily with past foreign policy issues. This applies even to Vietnam despite the persistence of the Nixon administration in a policy long since recognized by the American people as mistaken. However, the fourth essay is very different; it looks to the future and does so by examining the impact of science and technology on foreign affairs.

The Berlin Wall essay was read several times in draft by the Honorable E. Allan Lightner, Jr., who was Deputy Commandant and head of the State Department Mission in Berlin at the time the Wall was built. His criticisms and suggestions were invaluable to me in developing the essay to its present form. The comments of Professor Donald S. Detwiler, Southern Illinois University, were also very helpful. "The Cuba Missile Crisis" was read in draft by my colleague Professor Ward Morton who not only gave me several valuable suggestions, but also made many textual improvements. Helpful suggestions on the Vietnam piece were given me by Professors Detwiler and Charles Tenney, and by John C. Campbell of the Council on Foreign Relations, New York. The essay "The Continuing Revolution: Science, Technology, and Foreign Affairs" was read in draft by Professor I. L. (Jack) White, University of Oklahoma, and Professor Bertram Morris, University of Colorado; to both of them I am indebted for useful suggestions and textual improvements. The lecture on science, technology, and foreign affairs was given at a time when I was preparing to offer a graduate seminar on this subject. In this preparation I solicited the aid of many persons in the United States government and in academic circles. Were it not for the very generous response, I could not have proceeded with the lecture or the seminar. The names are too numerous for me to cite but I would like to express to them here my gratitude and appreciation.

The entire typing of the drafts and final manuscript was done by Jean Sykes to whom I am indebted, not only for her competence but also for her unfailing courtesy and cheerfulness.

Chapter 3, "Myths, Slogans, and Vietnam: Specious Abstraction and Foreign Policy" is an expanded and revised version of an article which appeared in the *Virginia Quarterly Review* 48, No. 1, Winter 1972.

HOWARD TRIVERS

Carbondale, Illinois
February 1972

1
The Berlin Wall

Kremlinology is a strange esoteric science. A primary method is textual exegesis, which is like biblical exegesis, interpretation of the Holy Script; only in this case the script isn't holy, but rather merely the printed texts of the day. It is very tedious, painstaking work; sometimes it can be very enlightening. Let me cite an example, not from Moscow but from another Communist regime, East Germany. After all, the methods of Kremlinology generally apply to most Communist regimes.

I was in Berlin at the time, in charge of the Eastern Affairs Section in the United States Mission Berlin, the State Department component of the headquarters of the U.S. commander in Berlin. On October 27, 1958, Walter Ulbricht, the head of the East German Communist Party, made a long speech at an election meeting, the full text of which was printed the next day in *Neues Deutschland,* the major party newspaper of East Germany. There were four American officers aside from myself in the Eastern Affairs Section, two of whom worked on political, and two on economic affairs. We also had four or five German employees. Our usual method of operation was to examine the East Berlin and the major East German provincial newspapers before a daily staff meeting at 9:30.

One of the German press analysts was Frau Strueck, who was primarily concerned with political matters; she had worked for the Americans in Berlin since 1945 and had come into the Eastern Affairs Section when it was established in 1949. She was a very acute, observant reader, who normally reported her findings to one of the junior officers. This October morning, she came directly to me as soon as I had arrived in the office before nine o'clock. There was a troubled expression on her face. "Mr. Trivers," she said, "will the Americans take my husband and me out of Berlin by airplane, if things go bad here?" She had been working for the Americans over twelve years, she explained. If the East German Communists took over the city, she would land in jail or Siberia. I knew her as a very calm person; this was quite unlike her. I asked her why she was so disturbed. "Look," she said, and she pointed to the text of Ulbricht's speech, three or four full newspaper pages in that morning's issue of *Neues Deutschland*. She had underlined with red pencil one word on one page, the word *neutralizieren*, that is, *neutralize*. Ulbricht had said, "We must neutralize West Berlin." She had been reading the German Communist press for nearly ten years; Ulbricht had never used that word before, nor had any other German Communist. It was ominous; it made her uneasy.

Fourteen days later, on November 10, 1958, in a speech at a reception in the Polish Embassy in Moscow given in honor of the Polish Party leader Gomulka, Khrushchev declared that the USSR was determined to end the Allied occupation of Berlin. On November 27, 1958, the Soviet Union delivered an ultimatum to the Western Allies demanding their withdrawal from West Berlin within six months, and the Berlin Crisis of 1958–1962 was started.

Frau Strueck's sensitive perception of the hidden

meaning in the seemingly innocuous word *neutralizieren* is an example of Kremlinology by exegesis. Of course, we sent a telegram to Washington reporting on this speech of Ulbricht, pointing out the novel use of the word *neutralize* and the ominous note, portending Soviet/East German action against West Berlin. Governments rarely react to such portents; presumably, weary German desk officers throughout the bureaucracy, leafing through their daily pile of telegrams, read the message and moved on to read the next one.

Nearly two years before this incident, in January 1957, during a visit to Moscow, Walter Ulbricht had reportedly proposed to Khrushchev and the Soviet leadership that a concerted Communist effort be made to drive the Western Powers out of West Berlin. He had argued that the East German Communist Party could not stabilize the situation in East Germany and properly develop East Germany economically and politically unless West Berlin, this open wound in the corpus of the Communist German Democratic Republic, could be taken over. Ulbricht's proposal had been rejected out of hand by Khrushchev. What had changed by the fall 1958? Several factors:

Khrushchev had consolidated his personal position in June 1957 by removing the opposition in the Politburo to his leadership, the so-called antiparty factional group, Molotov, Malenkov, Kaganovich, et al.; supported in this action by Marshall Zhukov, Khrushchev turned on him in November 1957, removing him from his position as Minister of Defense while Zhukov was on a trip to Yugoslavia.

The Soviet position in Eastern Europe, still uncertain in January 1957, after the Polish revolt in October 1956 and the Hungarian uprising October-November 1956 had been consolidated by fall 1958.

In August 1957 the Soviets launched successfully the first ICBM (Intercontinental Ballistic Missile), in October 1957, the first Sputnik (earth satellite). The Soviets, and Communists all over the world, hailed these achievements as representing a basic change in power relations. Hence the Soviets could now lead from a position of strength and within a framework of nuclear blackmail.

Once before the Soviets had tried to drive the Western Allies out of Berlin. Frustrated in his hopes to bring about the communization of all Germany after its defeat, Stalin imposed in the spring of 1948 a blockade on Berlin in order to force a withdrawal of the Western powers from Berlin. It was audacious, but Stalin was aware of the war weariness in the West, and the hasty demobilization of United States armed forces after the cessation of hostilities in 1945 must have outweighed in his mind the threat of American nuclear capability. In a sense, the airlift was a cowardly evasion; in July 1948 our Military Governor in Germany, General Lucius Clay, twice requested permission to attempt to break the surface blockade by sending an armored convoy from West Germany to Berlin. While we at the working level in the State Department supported him, the Joint Chiefs of Staff turned him down on the grounds that the United States did not then possess an adequate military posture to meet the consequences if hostilities with the Soviets were to ensue, even though the likelihood of such consequences were not regarded as great.

The airlift, however, succeeded, much to the surprise of the Soviets, and likewise to the surprise of most Western officials and planners. Let me interject a reminiscence at this point. In December 1947, after the London Council of Foreign Ministers meeting, the second CFM meeting dealing with a German peace settlement, had ended in a stalemate, Soviet Foreign Minister Molotov on his return trip to Moscow stopped over in East Berlin, apparently for consultations with the East German Communist leaders. This seemed very unusual to some of us at the working level in the State Department and indeed rather alarming. We thought that it might portend a Soviet blockade of Berlin. Hence we informally queried, in early January 1948, our friends in the Operations Division of the War Department as to the military capability for maintaining an airlift in support of West Berlin in the event of a Soviet blockade. A few weeks later we received a written reply to the effect that it would be possible to maintain the Allied garrisons by an airlift in the event of a Soviet blockade of military access on the surface routes, but that it would *not* be possible to sustain the two million West Berlin population by the airlift if the Soviets were to block civilian supply. There were not many military or civilian officials in the Western world who believed that the airlift would succeed so well in providing for the basic needs of the whole West Berlin population; certainly the Soviets expected it to fail. Had it not been for the determination of General Clay and the support of President Truman, "the captain with the mighty heart," the comprehensive Berlin airlift would never have been tried; had it not been for the talent of Generals LeMay and Tunner and the skill of the American and British fliers, it would not have succeeded.

For nearly ten years after the blockade the Soviets had suffered Western presence in Berlin, showing their discomfiture only by a persistent policy of minor harassment. Occasionally these harassments caused a flurry in the world press; often they went unnoticed; for Western officials they were a considerable part of the joy of life in West Berlin, pinpricks that kept one on constant alert. The Soviets had reason for their discomfiture. After

Soviet initiation of the Berlin crisis in November 1958, Khrushchev and the Communist press repeatedly termed West Berlin a "cancerous tumor" in the body politic of the Soviet bloc. West Berlin was an open hole 110 miles behind the Iron Curtain, an escape hatch. Free movement within the divided city made possible a continuous refugee flow from East Germany to West Germany. From 1945 to 1961 an estimated 3,300,000 Germans fled East Germany and East Berlin; more than 2,600,000 left since 1949 when West Berlin and the Federal German Republic began to keep records on the refugee flow. Since 1953 the border between East Germany and the Federal Republic has been dangerous for a refugee to try to cross, for the Communists guarded it with barbed wire, watchtowers with sharpshooters, and a "death strip" of plowed earth. Until August 1961, a refugee reaching East Berlin could cross to West Berlin on foot, by subway, or by the elevated railway—he was reasonably safe if he carried no large luggage and acted like a commuter. Consequently the bulk of the refugees from East Germany escaped by way of West Berlin from where they were carried by air to the German Federal Republic.

The ease in crossing from East Berlin to West Berlin made this also a favored route for defectors from Communist Eastern Europe. High officials from the Communist Eastern European countries would come to East Berlin for conferences and quietly slip across the border to West Berlin. An American intelligence officer went one afternoon on a shopping expedition to Kuerfuerstendamm, the main street in West Berlin. With the U.S. Army license, his car was identifiable as an American vehicle. When he returned to his parked car, he found a man there who in broken English asked if he could tell him where the Intelligence Office of the U.S. Army headquarters was in West Berlin. He was a high-ranking official from Bucharest who had been planning defection for many years and had come to attend a meeting in East Berlin. The American intelligence officer invited him into his car and took him where he wanted to go. Thereafter it became a joke among Western intelligence officers that the best way to establish contact with a high-ranking Eastern European defector was to go down to the Kudamm, park your car, and await his arrival. Facility of movement east to west and west to east made Berlin a major center for intelligence operations for both sides.

Easy access to West Berlin also meant at that time that West Berlin served as a "show window" of the Western world behind the Iron Curtain, both for East Germans and for Communist Eastern Europeans. The incomparably higher standard of living in West Berlin was manifest to East Berliners, East Germans, and Eastern Europeans. Furthermore, West Berlin had become a great cultural center, in education, theater, and music. In 1960 one-fourth of the students of the Free University of Berlin came from East Germany and East Berlin. That same year East Berliners and East Germans borrowed 250,000 books from West Berlin libraries, bought 560,000 tickets to West Berlin theaters and operas, and ten million admissions to West Berlin movie houses. Furthermore, the free radio transmitters in West Berlin were a great annoyance to the Soviets and the East German Communists, particularly RIAS (Radio in the American Sector) which not only carried information about the free world but also provided factual information about the Communist countries, often otherwise denied the peoples behind the Iron Curtain. RIAS had a very large audience in East Germany, but it also had listeners in Czechoslovakia and Poland as well. It is easy to understand why the Communists regarded an accessible West Berlin as a major impediment to the consolidation of the Soviet and Communist position in East Germany and Eastern Europe.

Lenin had said that he who controls Germany controls Europe; he had expected the Bolshevik Revolution to be followed by a Communist revolution in Germany. Indeed he did not believe initially that communism in Russia could survive without an associated Communist revolution in Germany. Since Lenin, Soviet thinking had invariably included the concept of a great revolutionary alliance with Germany. From the very outset of World War II, the Soviets made a distinction in their policy and propaganda between the German people and the Nazi government. Stalin's famous order of the day to the Red Army February 23, 1943, after Stalingrad, stated that it is a wicked, malicious libel that the Red Army aims at the destruction of the German people. In Stalin's words, "History teaches that Hitlers come and go but the German people and the German state remain." The Soviets, as a result, sifted and indoctrinated German prisoners of war and organized a Free Germany Committee and the affiliated German Officers Union at Moscow in July 1943. At the outset of occupation the Soviets could thus rely not only on the native Communists in their occupation zone but also on the cadre of German Communists who had spent the Hitler period in exile, many in the Soviet Union, and on the new converts from the German prisoners of war. The Soviets came into occupation thus prepared to set up in their zone under ostensible German leadership a regime of the desired familiar pattern.

It was the French in the Allied Control Council, 1945–48, who thwarted the fulfillment of the Potsdam Agreement provision stipulating that certain essential central German administrative departments, headed by a state secretary, should be established, particularly in the fields of finance, transport, communications, foreign trade, and industry; such departments to act under the direction of the Control Council. The French believed that such central German departments, headed by Germans, should not be established prior to a decision on the German political structure and that their reconstitution prior to such decisions might prejudge the form of the ultimate German political establishment. Accordingly, the French representative in the Allied Control Council persistently refused to proceed with the implementation of the provision for central German departments as formulated at Potsdam. He offered alternative suggestions, that agencies be established headed by Allied representatives, for example, but these alternatives invariably found the Russians insisting that the word and letter of the Potsdam Agreement be fulfilled. It is certainly true that the Russians hid nicely behind the French on this matter, since Soviet policy in the Eastern zone was from the start incompatible with the treatment of Germany as an economic unit and the effective operation in Germany of central German agencies in the economic fields. Nevertheless, it is intriguing to speculate as to what the course of development might have been if the French had not adopted such a strong position. I do not mean to imply that the Control Council would have functioned adequately and that our problems in Germany would have been solved if the central German agencies had been established. On the contrary, it is not unlikely that central agencies formed right after Potsdam might have become so infiltrated and covertly controlled by German Communists that their incorporation in a reestablished central German government would have given the Soviets an immediate advantage in the ensuing internal struggle for Communist domination of German political life.

As a result of the French position, Germany from

the summer of 1945 through 1946 came to be governed in separate zonal compartments under the unilateral administration of the respective zone commanders. Such a state of affairs was obviously intolerable; in particular, the failure to treat Germany as a single economic unit brought about a requirement for large-scale importation of foodstuffs into Western Germany, placing an extraordinary financial burden on the United States and Great Britain. To break the deadlock, the United States government, first at a meeting of the Council of Foreign Ministers in Paris on July 11, 1946, and immediately thereafter at the Allied Control Council in Berlin on July 20, 1946, offered to join its zone economically with that of any other occupying power. The British accepted this proposal; the Soviets rejected it because it was not properly based on the Potsdam Agreement; the French likewise refused to accept it. The administrative union of the British and American zones for economic purposes was made fully effective on January 1, 1947. Subsequently the French in 1949 joined their zone to the American and British zones. Developments leading to the unity of Western Germany and the establishment of the Federal Republic have all ensued as a consequence of the British acceptance of this United States offer in 1946. The Soviets rejected this offer, just as they had previously rejected proposals made by the United States representative in the Control Council that German administrative agencies be set up for the United States, British, and Soviet zones, on the alleged ground of French unwillingness to establish central agencies for the four zones. If the Soviets had really wanted to implement political and economic unity for Germany, they could have done so. Sensing scant opportunity at the time to achieve Communist domination over all Germany, the Soviets preferred to maintain exclusive unilateral control over their own zone.

There are many reasons why the Soviets made this decision, holding tenaciously to their position in the Soviet zone and transforming it into a Communist state, the German Democratic Republic (GDR). In the first place, from the standpoint of traditional military thinking, East Germany was a valuable addition to the glacis which thus stretched from the Western frontier of the USSR across Eastern Europe to the Elbe.

Second, the massive Soviet occupation forces in East Germany served as a "cork in the bottle" with respect to the political instabilities in Eastern Europe. When Khrushchev and other Soviet Politburo members descended on Warsaw in October 1956 to attempt to prevent the accession of Gomulka to the top Polish Communist party leadership position, five divisions of the Soviet Army in East Germany fanned out along the East German-Polish frontier to add to the threat of the two Soviet divisions marching on Warsaw from their barracks in lower Silesia. When twelve years later in August 1968 the Soviets invaded Czechoslovakia, major components of the Soviet invading force came from the Soviet Army in East Germany.

Third, East Germany makes a very important economic contribution to the Soviet Union. For many years East Germany has been the number one trade partner of the USSR, having around 20 percent of total Soviet foreign trade—in 1970 it was 23 percent. The GDR provides the Soviets and the Eastern European Communist countries with high quality products: machine tools, electrical equipment, optical and chemical products.

Fourth, a divided Germany is a weakened Germany. However, while West Germany alone is certainly no threat to the Soviet Union, even a reunited Germany would hardly be a serious threat.

Fifth, the Soviets regard their strong position in East Germany as a potential jumping-off place against

West Germany and against Western Europe, both in a military and a political warfare sense. While in recent years the Soviets have muted their aggressive language in view of their efforts to achieve recognition, *de facto* or *de jure*, of the GDR and general acceptance of the *status quo* in central and eastern Europe, nevertheless it is doubtful that the Soviets have abandoned the long-range aim of unifying Germany under Communist control. For this purpose the GDR is a vantage point or springboard. In a speech at the All-German Workers Conference in Leipzig on March 7, 1959, Khrushchev made clear his expectation that Germany will be reunited in the future, when the working class in West Germany also comes to power and brings about "the socioeconomic reforms" which will make it possible to put the two parts of Germany readily together again. He said, "how, on what foundation shall the reunification of Germany take place? We are not for just any kind of reunification . . . one must approach the question of reunification above all from the class standpoint. Those who represent the interest of the working class cannot even permit the thought that by a reunification of Germany the workers and peasants of the German Democratic Republic . . . shall lose all their achievements and agree to live as formerly under the conditions of the capitalist yoke. . . . I repeat we are for the reunification of Germany and the German people will again be reunited. This is only a question of time. In this connection it is naturally very important on what foundation Germany will again be reunited." [1]

In the note of November 27, 1958,[2] the Soviet government declared that it regarded as null and void all the wartime agreements on the occupation of Germany and the administration of Berlin. It demanded the withdrawal of Western military forces from the city and proposed to make West Berlin a demilitarized "free city," although "the most correct and natural" solution would be to reunite West Berlin with East Berlin and to absorb it into the German Democratic Republic. If the Western allies did not accept this proposal within six months, the Soviet Union would at that time sign a peace treaty with the German Democratic Republic and turn over to the East Germans control of all access to Berlin. Thus the Soviets sought to "normalize" the situation in Berlin, and "only madmen" would think of "unleashing another world war over the preservation of privileges of occupiers in West Berlin." While Stalin had attacked the Allied position in Berlin quietly with practical blockade measures, Khrushchev attacked the position with diplomatic notes, bombastic speeches, the illogic of Communist rationalization, and threats of war. Although the Russians were obviously the aggressors in the blockade, Khrushchev's note of November 27 put the West on the defensive to explain why such apparently "reasonable" proposals aiming to eliminate an "abnormal" remnant of World War II were not acceptable. More importantly, if the Soviets were actually to turn over access controls to Berlin to the East German authorities and the arrangements were unacceptable to the Western Allies, then we would have been obliged to take positive actions which might appear aggressive in order to maintain free access to Berlin.

The United States' reply of December 31, 1958,[3] rejected the Soviet allegations and demands and stated that it could not embark on discussions with the Soviet Union "under menace or ultimatum." It closed by inquiring whether the Soviet Union would be ready to enter into discussions among the four powers on the question of Berlin "in the wider framework of negotiations for solution of the German problem as well as that of European security." Moscow responded on January 10, 1959, with the proposal for a peace conference and summit talks on Berlin and Germany, with participation by the German Democratic Republic and the Federal Republic of Germany. It did not withdraw the six-month deadline; it chose not to mention it. Eager for negotiations, without the duress explicitly having been withdrawn, the Western powers on February 16 [4] informed the Soviet government that they were prepared to take part in a four-power conference of foreign ministers to deal with the problem of Germany in all its aspects. They likewise agreed that German "advisers" be invited and consulted.

The foreign ministers conference opened in Geneva on May 11, 1959. Thereby the Soviets achieved two gains: first, the conference was beginning within the six-month deadline of the November 27 ultimatum, and, secondly, East Germans were in attendance as if they represented a legitimate government. These Geneva negotiations are a sad story, for the Western powers offered such concessions to the Soviets that, if their proposals had been accepted, the position of West Berlin would probably have been undermined. The following concessions were offered in the Allied proposals of June 16: [5]

1. The Western garrisons were to be limited to their present figure, approximately 11,000, and they would be armed wholly with conventional weapons as at the time. Consideration would be given to the reduction of the size of the garrisons "if developments in the situation permit."

2. Free and unrestricted access to West Berlin should be continued under the procedures in effect in April 1959, but these procedures might be carried out by East German personnel.

3. "Activities which might either disturb public order or seriously affect the rights and interests, or amount to interference in the internal affairs, of others [propa-